N. T. WRIGHT
FOR EVERYONE
BIBLE STUDY GUIDES

1 CORINTHIANS

13 STUDIES FOR INDIVIDUALS AND GROUPS

N. T. WRIGHT

WITH DALE & SANDY LARSEN

IVP Connect

An imprint of InterVarsity Press
Downers Grove, Illinois

InterVarsity Press
P.O. Box 1400, Downers Grove, IL 60515-1426
World Wide Web: www.ivpress.com
E-mail: email@ivpress.com

This study guide is based on and includes excerpts adapted from Paul for Everyone: 1 Corinthians, ©2003, 2004 Nicholas Thomas Wright. All Scripture quotations, unless otherwise indicated, are taken from the New Testament for Everyone. Copyright ©2001-2008 by Nicholas Thomas Wright. Used by permission of SPCK, London. All rights reserved.

InterVarsity Press® is the book-publishing division of InterVarsity Christian Fellowship/USA®, a movement of students and faculty active on campus at hundreds of universities, colleges and schools of nursing in the United States of America, and a member movement of the International Fellowship of Evangelical Students. For information about local and regional activities, write Public Relations Dept., InterVarsity Christian Fellowship/USA, 6400 Schroeder Rd., P.O. Box 7895, Madison, WI 53707-7895, or visit the IVCF website at <www.intervarsity.org>.

Cover design: Cindy Kiple
Cover image: Photos.com / Jupiter Images
Interior image: Clipart.com

ISBN 978-0-8308-2187-7

Printed in the United States of America ∞

P	18	17	16	15	14	13	12	11	10	9	8	7	6	5	4	3	2
Y	24	23	22	21	20	19	18	17	16	15	14	13					

CONTENTS

GETTING THE MOST
OUT OF 1 CORINTHIANS

In the first century, Corinth was a lively seaport in Greece, not far from Athens. People and cultures of every sort jostled together, just like so many places in today's world. The young church there was as lively as the place itself, with as many questions and problems—as much joy and excitement—as any growing church today. Paul's pastoral sensitivity and deep insight come together to make this letter one of his crowning achievements, full of good things for us to ponder and enjoy today.

The city of Corinth had been destroyed by the Romans in 146 B.C., and rebuilt by Julius Caesar in 44 B.C. as a Roman colony. Since that time, about a hundred years before this letter was written, Corinth had prided itself on being a Roman city on Greek soil. It celebrated its Roman style of buildings, its Roman culture, its special links to the capital of a worldwide empire. It also prided itself on its intellectual life.

Most of the Christians in Corinth had not been Jews but ordinary "pagans." They had been Gentiles, believing in various gods and goddesses, but without any idea that history, the story of the world, was *going* anywhere, or that their own lives might be part of that forward movement. Again and again Paul wants them to learn this lesson: that they have been caught up into a great movement of the love and power of the one true God, the God of Israel, whose work for the whole world had now been unveiled through the events concerning his Son. That's why Jesus is at the center of the picture Paul paints.

That was the message Paul first brought to Corinth when he founded the church there in midcentury. But Paul hadn't been the only teacher they'd had in the city. Not long after he'd gone, a wonderful speaker, greatly learned in Scripture and able to explain it powerfully, had arrived. His name was Apollos, and he came from Alexandria in Egypt, where there was a strong Jewish community which included a great Jewish philosopher by the name of Philo. Apollos met some of Paul's colleagues in Ephesus (see Acts 18:24-28) and later went to Corinth (see Acts 18:27—19:1). Paul wrote his letter to the Corinthians from Ephesus while Apollos was probably still in Corinth. (For more on this letter, also see my *Paul for Everyone: 1 Corinthians,* on which this guide is based, published by SPCK and Westminster John Knox.)

In the time since Paul left Corinth after founding the church there (see Acts 18:18), various problems and questions had arisen. So the church sent a delegation consisting of Stephanas, Fortunatus and Achaicus with a letter, asking Paul to respond and give his counsel. This he did, and the result is the letter we have in 1 Corinthians.

SUGGESTIONS FOR INDIVIDUAL STUDY

1. As you begin each study, pray that God will speak to you through his Word.

2. Read the introduction to the study and respond to the "Open" question that follows it. This is designed to help you get into the theme of the study.

3. Read and reread the Bible passage to be studied. Each study is designed to help you consider the meaning of the passage in its context. The commentary and questions in this guide are based on my own translation of each passage found in the companion volume to this guide in the For Everyone series on the New Testament (published by SPCK and Westminster John Knox).

4. Write your answers to the questions in the spaces provided or in a personal journal. Each study includes three types of questions: obser-

vation questions, which ask about the basic facts in the passage; interpretation questions, which delve into the meaning of the passage; and application questions, which help you discover the implications of the text for growing in Christ. Writing out your responses can bring clarity and deeper understanding of yourself and of God's Word.

5. Each session features selected comments from the For Everyone series. These notes provide further biblical and cultural background and contextual information. They are designed not to answer the questions for you but to help you along as you study the Bible for yourself. For even more reflections on each passage, you may wish to have on hand a copy of the companion volume from the For Everyone series as you work through this study guide.

6. Use the guidelines in the "Pray" section to focus on God, thanking him for what you have learned and praying about the applications that have come to mind.

SUGGESTIONS FOR GROUP MEMBERS

1. Come to the study prepared. Follow the suggestions for individual study mentioned above. You will find that careful preparation will greatly enrich your time spent in group discussion.

2. Be willing to participate in the discussion. The leader of your group will not be lecturing. Instead, she or he will be asking the questions found in this guide and encouraging the members of the group to discuss what they have learned.

3. Stick to the topic being discussed. These studies focus on a particular passage of Scripture. Only rarely should you refer to other portions of the Bible or outside sources. This allows for everyone to participate on equal ground and for in-depth study.

4. Be sensitive to the other members of the group. Listen attentively when they describe what they have learned. You may be surprised by their insights! Each question assumes a variety of answers. Many questions do not have "right" answers, particularly questions that

aim at meaning or application. Instead the questions push us to explore the passage more thoroughly.

When possible, link what you say to the comments of others. Also, be affirming whenever you can. This will encourage some of the more hesitant members of the group to participate.

5. Be careful not to dominate the discussion. We are sometimes so eager to express our thoughts that we leave too little opportunity for others to respond. By all means participate! But allow others to also.

6. Expect God to teach you through the passage being discussed and through the other members of the group. Pray that you will have an enjoyable and profitable time together, but also that as a result of the study you will find ways that you can take action individually and/ or as a group.

7. It will be helpful for groups to follow a few basic guidelines. These guidelines, which you may wish to adapt to your situation, should be read at the beginning of the first session.

- Anything said in the group is considered confidential and will not be discussed outside the group unless specific permission is given to do so.

- We will provide time for each person present to talk if he or she feels comfortable doing so.

- We will talk about ourselves and our own situations, avoiding conversation about other people.

- We will listen attentively to each other.

- We will be very cautious about giving advice.

Additional suggestions for the group leader can be found at the back of the guide.

GOD'S STRANGE WISDOM

1 Corinthians 1:1—3:4

People give themselves away by what they go on talking about, almost to the point of obsession. It doesn't take long in someone's company, or even in a phone call, before you discover what's really exciting them, what is at the center of their waking thoughts.

If we had any doubts about what Paul was excited about, the first paragraph of 1 Corinthians, one of his most varied and lengthy letters, would soon put us straight. One name keeps coming up over and over again like a motif in an opera. It's good to remind ourselves where Paul's heart lay, because we can easily read the whole letter merely as an argumentative tract, almost bossy sometimes, setting the Corinthians right about this and that as though his only concern was to whip them into shape. It wasn't. His central concern here and throughout his life and work was quite simply Jesus.

OPEN

How would you describe a mature person?

STUDY

1. *Read 1 Corinthians 1:1-17.* How does Paul demonstrate in 1:1-9 that Christ is involved in the Corinthians' past, present and future?

2. On what basis were the Corinthian Christians creating divisions, and why was this so destructive (1:10-17)?

Go to any church where two preachers have worked side by side or in quick succession, and you will find people comparing them. That's natural, but how easily it can pass into factions and rivalry. It's a sobering thought that the church faced such division in its very earliest years. People sometimes talk as if first-generation Christianity enjoyed a pure, untroubled honeymoon period, after which things became more difficult; but there's no evidence for this in the New Testament. Right from the start Paul found himself not only announcing the gospel of Jesus but struggling to hold together in a single family those who had obeyed its summons.

3. What issues do churches divide over today, and with what negative results?

4. *Read 1 Corinthians 1:18-31.* Why does the wisdom of God appear foolish to the world?

5. "Who and what you now are is a gift from God in King Jesus
   . . . so that, as the Bible puts it, 'Anyone who boasts should boast in
   the Lord'" (1:30-31). In what practical ways can we express that our
   status and self-esteem are not from ourselves but instead from the
   Lord?

6. *Read 1 Corinthians 2:1-13.* How would you characterize Paul's approach to the Corinthians in 2:1-5?

7. Think about those people who persuaded you or helped you to first
   put your faith in Christ. How did they (perhaps unknowingly) follow Paul's example with the Corinthians?

The deepest mysteries of human life—love, death, joy, beauty and
the rest—have for millennia been believed to point to the deepest
mystery of them all, the mystery of God. Among the writings of
ancient Israel, both in the Bible and in other books, many try to
penetrate to this truth, to discover what is going on in God's world,
and where different people might fit into his purposes. Paul picks up
the Jewish tradition and declares that God's past, present and future
have at last been unveiled in and through Jesus the Messiah.

8. Why did the rulers of Jesus' time fail to understand who Jesus was
   (2:6-13)?

According to Paul, world history divides into two ages or epochs. There is the *present age,* the period of history characterized by human rebellion, sin, despair and death. Then there is the *age to come,* the time when the one true God will be king over all the world, bringing to an end the rule of all forces that oppose him. And the *age to come* has already broken into the present age in Jesus the Messiah.

9. How would you identify a *mature* Christian?

10. Hearing Paul's letter to this point, the Corinthians were perhaps glad that Paul seemed to have forgotten or left behind the issue he started with in verse 10, fighting among factions in the church. If so they were in for a shock, because the discussion about wisdom and maturity was preparing the way to come back to the point.

     Read 1 Corinthians 2:14—3:4. Why does strife among Christians reflect spiritual immaturity?

     Paul's point here deserves reflection in today's church as we so easily lapse from serious issues to personality clashes and from personalities to mere gossip, while all the time pretending we are still dealing with important matters.

11. If freedom from jealousy and quarreling (3:3) is a mark of Christian maturity, how would you evaluate your own maturity in Christ?

12. By the same standard, how mature is your church or Christian fellowship?

PRAY

Where do you feel you especially need "the mind of the Messiah" (1 Corinthians 2:16)? Pray about those issues, looking for the wisdom of Christ as you do so.

THE SOLE FOUNDATION

1 Corinthians 3:5-23

Was Paul the "founder" of Christianity? The debate comes and goes. From time to time people try to establish that Jesus didn't really begin Christianity, and that what we know as Christianity and project back onto Jesus was in fact the invention of Paul. There is a sense in which Paul did found churches (as he did at Corinth), like somebody laying the foundation of a building. He was happy to describe his work in that way. But the foundation he put down was Jesus himself, the Messiah, the Lord. That is the only foundation there ever can be.

OPEN

What are some faulty foundations on which people try to build their lives? What happens as a result?

STUDY

1. Paul has no basic quarrel with Apollos, the gifted speaker who ministered in Corinth after Paul left there (Acts 18:24-28). He does have

a problem with the idea that anyone might play him and Apollos against one another.

Read 1 Corinthians 3:5-23. What different roles for servants of Christ does Paul mention in verses 5-11?

2. Here Paul uses two metaphors for work in God's kingdom: a farm and a building. The images seem quite different from each other. What similarities do they share?

To use a different metaphor, Paul and Apollos are simply the people who serve the food, while God is responsible for choosing it and cooking it. You shouldn't make a fuss about which waiter brings the food to your table. What matters is that God is in charge in the kitchen.

3. What are some ways that people rank different kinds of Christian service as more or less important?

4. Why do you think we look on them in that way?

There is only one pedestal in the kingdom of God and only one person to be put on it. But it isn't a statue to be put up as a monument in a town square. It is a cross; and the Messiah who hung and died on it passed judgment on all human fame, celebrity, popularity and reputation.

5. How can Paul's comments in 3:5-11 help us curb rival factions in the church?

6. In 3:12-17 what makes the difference in the two outcomes of the test by fire?

The building materials Paul mentions in verse 12 were things you might use to adorn or build up one particular building: the temple in Jerusalem. Just as God's own presence dwelt in Solomon's temple, so God's Spirit dwells within the Christian community, making them the functional equivalent of the temple within the new dispensation, the "age to come" that has already arrived.

7. As you think about your own Christian community, what does it mean that "you are God's temple" (v. 16)?

8. The main point of this passage is the seriousness with which Paul takes the various tasks and responsibilities of Christians, particularly leaders and teachers in the church. We are not playing games. There are serious and lasting issues at stake. It is possible to build

wisely and well and with the right materials. It is also possible to build badly or with the wrong materials.

Think about your leadership responsibilities, whether in the church, home, community, workplace or any other setting. What is at stake for the people you lead and for yourself?

9. In what ways might you need to take your leadership role more seriously?

When the "fire" does its work, Paul says, builders who have used the wrong material will "suffer loss," but they themselves will still be saved. This seems to be Paul's way of preserving his view of Christian assurance while maintaining also a serious view of Christian responsibility for what one does with the new life which begins, as the Spirit's gift, with faith and baptism.

10. Consider Paul's statement in 3:18. When have you had to discard the wisdom of the world in order to be open to receive God's wisdom?

The pressure of the world around us is always trying to make us either deny that we know anything or adopt a brittle, high-risk, know-it-all position. Genuine Christian faith is a combination of humility and confidence, which is hard to keep in balance.

11. How does Paul emphasize the present significance and future role of
    Christians in verses 21-23?

Christians are already resurrection people because of the sure hope
that is theirs through the gospel message of Jesus' own resurrection
(which Paul will affirm in 1 Corinthians 15). The present and the
future belong to them; that's how important they already are. They
are assured, even while the present evil age is continuing, that they
belong in the age to come. Nor do they belong in it as extras in a
script that is basically about someone or something else. They are
the stars of the show!

12. Consider the vast areas which Paul names in verse 22—the world,
    life, death, the present, the future. What does it mean for you that it
    is now *yours* because you belong to Christ?

PRAY

Paul began this section of his letter by warning the Corinthians not
to deceive themselves. Pray that you will neither deceive yourself nor
let others deceive you. Pray that you will not waste time and energy in
works that will only burn up, but that your works will last, built with
good materials on the foundation of Christ.

Puffed Up or Powerful?

1 Corinthians 4:1-21

Some religious systems try to make out that the world isn't so bad after all, or alternatively that what we perceive as evil is just an illusion. In Judaism and Christianity, the world is God's good and lovely world, and evil is a real, powerful and horrible intruder into it. Sooner or later God must and will put it right. Believing in God's final judgment is part of believing that God is the good and wise Creator and that his kingdom will one day come on earth as in heaven. But it's very tempting for people to want to put everything right and to pay off what they see as old scores ahead of time. We think we know what God should do, and we're eager to give him advice.

The Corinthian Christians seem to think that their new status in Christ, coupled with the "wisdom" they think they have in the world's eyes, gives them the right to pass judgment on people, including Paul himself. Paul's response is: when judgment comes, it will bring to light a lot of other things as well as his own apostolic shortcomings, if such there be. Maybe it will also show up something about the Corinthians' intentions.

OPEN

What or whom do you wish God would judge now rather than waiting for some future day of judgment? Why might God's judgment be delayed?

STUDY

1. *Read 1 Corinthians 4:1-21.* After three chapters of introduction, we have a sense that here at last Paul has arrived at the real confrontation which needs to take place. Why does Paul say in 4:1-5 that he isn't that concerned with the judgment or criticism he might receive from people?

2. Apostles are like household managers whose job is to look after the silverware and administer the domestic accounts. God's mysteries (1 Corinthians 2:7) are like a rich storehouse of treasures to be used appropriately. Apostles and teachers don't own the treasure; they merely have to do what they're told with it. What is required is simply that they be faithful with what has been entrusted to them.

   Why should the Corinthians themselves, as well as we ourselves, be careful about the criticisms we lodge against others?

3. Of course this principle would be easy to abuse. Most of us know of ministers who have refused all discipline or correction and have brazenly asserted their innocence when everyone else can see their folly or guilt. Indeed in 1 Corinthians 5 Paul makes quite clear that

in some instances the church must bring God's future judgment into the present.

When to listen to whispers of criticism and when to dismiss them as irrelevant and time-wasting—these are decisions which need wisdom and good judgment. What or who can help us discern how to evaluate criticism of ourselves or those in church leadership?

4. In verse 9 Paul draws the picture of a Roman general returning to the city after winning a great victory. The Roman army would march in parade through the streets and pass under a triumphal arch, carrying the booty they had captured. At the back of the procession came a bedraggled and weary gang of prisoners. Usually the day would end with the prisoners being killed or sold into slavery. It was a public display of glory, power and victory, a celebration of the fact that Rome had triumphed again.

Where does Paul place himself in such a procession, and what does that say about Christian leadership in ministry?

5. How in 4:6-13 do you see the crucified Messiah as Paul's model for ministry?

6. If Paul needed to make this point to the Christians in Corinth, what do you think he would say to comfortable Western Christians today?

7. The word translated "puffed up" is a favorite in this letter of Paul. After all he has to say about humility, why does he tell the Corinthians to "copy me" (v. 16)?

8. When have you seen a stark difference between talk and power (v. 20)?

9. What does this passage say about how authority should be exercised in the church?

10. For centuries church leaders have copied the models of authority in the surrounding world, whether autocratic or democratic. What dangers are inherent in the church imitating the world's patterns of authority?

Paul had no intention of telling the Corinthians to take a vote about what sort of church they wanted. But neither was he going to bully or browbeat them from a great height. His only authority—but it is the most powerful sort—was that of someone who was living and preaching the gospel of Jesus and acting out the commission which Jesus had given him.

11. How would you summarize the main points Paul makes in this chapter about what our attitudes should be toward those in Christian leadership?

PRAY

Pray for the leaders of your church, that God will give them wisdom, protect them from temptation and keep them faithful to him. Pray for your own attitude toward church leaders, that you will not judge them (or their critics or their defenders) prematurely but that you will also exercise discernment about sin and righteousness.

CONDUCT IN THE BODY

1 Corinthians 5:1—6:20

Wwe stood in line for the ride at the carnival. But as we got closer I saw a sign. This ride was for children only. Beside the sign was a small wooden archway, and you had to walk through it without stooping in order to get to the ride. Only people who could walk through were allowed on. Anybody else simply wouldn't fit. Two of my children got on (with an anxious backward glance at me) but I had to stay out.

God's kingdom isn't a carnival ride, but the same principle applies. The Creator God has unveiled his genuine model for humanity in Jesus the Messiah, and there are certain ways of behaving which just won't fit. If you want to be truly, fully human, those ways of behaving have to be left behind.

OPEN

What changes of behavior has God led you to make (or perhaps is still leading you to make) because you belong to Christ? Why are your new patterns of behavior a better reflection of the life of Christ?

STUDY

1. *Read 1 Corinthians 5:1-13.* This passage raises two issues which we shall be looking at over the next three chapters as Paul moves from one topic to another, mostly involving questions about sex. First, where the lines regarding sexual behavior are to be drawn, and second, what kind of discipline is appropriate in cases of severe misbehavior.

   What was the sex scandal in the Corinthian church and why was it so outrageous (5:1)?

2. How had the church itself responded to this man living with (presumably) his stepmother, and why does this concern Paul even more (5:2)?

3. Paul uses the phrase "the satan" sparingly; it is a Jewish term for the devil and indicates the one who accuses people of wrongdoing and entices them to evil so he will have something to accuse them of. To put someone out of the community is to expel them from the sphere of the Messiah and send them back into the sphere in which the satan holds sway.

   Why do you think Paul urges the church to take such extreme disciplinary measures against the offender?

4. What harm is done to a church body when they tolerate open sin among their members?

5. At the first Passover, when the Jewish people came out of Egypt in the exodus, they had to hurry. They baked bread without the normal yeast, or leaven, which they used to make it rise, so they could cook it quickly, carry it easily and eat it in a hurry. Paul isn't just using an image drawn at random in 1 Corinthians 5:6-8. At the first Passover in Egypt each family slaughtered a lamb and put its blood on the doorposts of the house so the angel of death would pass over them. When Jews of Paul's day kept the Passover festival, they sacrificed lambs in the temple. It was no coincidence that Jesus died and rose again at Passover time; he was the real Passover lamb and his death won deliverance for the whole world. The whole Christian life, from this point of view, becomes one long Passover celebration! And at this Passover there must be no "leaven of the old life"—the kind of behavior that pagans engage in and that Christians can be lured back into if they aren't careful.

How are churches in the Western world likely to respond to engaging in the kind of discipline Paul describes?

Just as Israel was commanded not to tolerate evil in its midst (Deuteronomy 17:7, which Paul quotes in 5:13), so the church must see wickedness for what it is, a cancer which will spread if it is not cut out at the first sign. The Christian community has the God-given right and duty to discriminate between those who are living in the Messiah's way and those who are not.

6. *Read 1 Corinthians 6:1-20.* What is Paul's reasoning for forbidding Christians to take each other to court (6:1-8)?

7. From time to time in our own day it happens that church people, sometimes those in leadership, are taken to court by one another. It gets into the newspapers and all the gossips have a field day at the church's expense. A public dispute between Christians is a sign that Christians are really no different from everybody else. And 1 Corinthians is all about the fact that Christians *are* different from everybody else, and if they're not, they might as well not bother calling themselves Christians in the first place.

Where in the church—even in your church—are we behaving in such a way that we are shaming the gospel in the eyes of the world?

8. Many in today's world have drunk so deeply from the "anything goes" culture that they find the mere suggestion of moral restrictions on sexual behavior (such as those mentioned in 6:9-11) surprising or even offensive. Paul is not suggesting that sexual error is worse than any other kind. Nor is he saying that God has an arbitrary list of rules and if you break them you won't get in. It is rather that his kingdom will be peopled by humans who reflect his image completely; and behavior in the present which distorts and defaces that image leads in the opposite direction.

How, even on a human level, is sexual permissiveness often destructive to people and relationships?

9. We often speak of faith in Christ in terms of *spiritual life*. How does Paul emphasize in 6:12-20 that the Christian's relationship with Jesus is not simply spiritual but physical as well?

10. How does this passage challenge the idea of "casual sex"?

11. Paul says, "Run away from immorality" (6:18). What form should this "running away" look like for Christians today?

12. As you look over chapters 5 and 6, what warnings and what assurances do you find?

PRAY

"You were quite an expensive purchase! So glorify God in your body" (6:20). Paul clearly refers to the cross, where Jesus paid the price of his own life, his own blood, to rescue sinners. Thank the Lord for paying the ultimate price for you. Reflect on your worth in his eyes. Ask him to show you any ways in which you are not glorifying him with your body, and pray for the grace to make the changes you need to make.

5

MARRIAGE AND RELATED MATTERS

1 Corinthians 7:1-40

We must not make the mistake of thinking that the apostle Paul lived in a world that was morally like the world of our parents and grandparents. It was more like the Western world today than like that of the mid-twentieth century. Especially in the upper levels of the social scale, divorce and remarriage were common; and there was strong social pressure, sometimes even legal pressure, for divorced or widowed people, especially women, to remarry quickly. With increasing mobility on the one hand and the huge changes brought about by the Christian gospel on the other, church members must have found themselves faced with a bewildering array of moral questions and difficulties, made harder by pressures from some Christians who said that sexual relations, even within marriage, were a poor second best to a life of abstinence. This is the minefield Paul picks his way through in this passage.

OPEN

What would you say promotes holy living?

STUDY

1. The idea of mutual equality between husband and wife was daring in Paul's time and is still challenging today. *Read 1 Corinthians 7:1-16.* How does Paul express the idea of mutual equality in practical terms?

2. While some in the Corinthian church were all for casting off moral restraint altogether (1 Corinthians 6:12), others were all for moral severity. In line with some of the well-known philosophies of the time, they were urging people either to celibacy or to abstain from sexual relations within marriage as the way to new depths of personal holiness and spiritual maturity.

   What is Paul's response to this idea?

   Paul is quite clear that being celibate is a perfectly good state, providing one is in control of one's sexual impulses. Unlike many in our world, he doesn't consider life without active sexual relations to be inferior or deficient. He doesn't disagree with celibacy itself; he disagrees with the use to which he knows it's being put in Corinth. To be married but to abstain from sexual relations is to ask for trouble.

3. In verses 8-16 Paul divides his comments into three areas: a message for people who have been married but now aren't (vv. 8-9), a message for married people (vv. 10-11), and a message for people in the tricky situation of being married to someone who is not a Christian (vv. 12-16).

What should determine an unmarried Christian's choice about whether to marry (vv. 8-9)?

In verses 8-9 it's quite likely that Paul is referring to widows and widowers rather than to those who have never married, since he gives advice later in the chapter to those who have not been married (vv. 25-38). He is walking a tightrope here between the social pressures toward remarriage on the one hand and the pressures from some "spiritual" teachers toward permanent celibacy on the other. He wants the Corinthians to be free from the pressure to get married again; there is much to be said for being able to choose to remarry or not, without outside forces influencing their choice. This was quite a socially subversive, even shocking suggestion in Paul's world. But equally he wants them to be comfortable and not ashamed in the face of those advocating abstinence, to admit to themselves that their sexual desires are still powerful and will be a nuisance and a temptation if they do not marry.

4. In verse 10 Paul refers to a specific command of Jesus himself, presumably the one we find in Mark 10:9 and similar passages. What sorts of behavior by husbands and wives will help *prevent* the desire for divorce?

5. In the early church it must have often happened that one marriage partner would hear and believe the gospel while the other did not. While here permitting divorce if an unbelieving spouse wants to separate (v. 15), Paul will urge in verse 39 and in 2 Corinthians 6:14 that Christians should marry only other Christians. What would be

the potential value of a believer choosing to remain with an unbelieving spouse (vv. 12-16)?

6. *Read 1 Corinthians 7:17-31.* We may wonder why Paul is talking about circumcision and slavery in the middle of a chapter on marriage and sex. He is using them to illustrate the larger point he is making, which we find repeated three times here: don't try to change the status you had when you became a Christian.

   What sudden and impulsive life changes might a person tend to make when he or she becomes a Christian?

7. What point does Paul make about social status in the world's eyes in 7:17-24?
   _" Is there a correlation between god's Law of Love's Compassion and church rules...."

8. Paul most likely left Corinth in A.D. 51. Right around that time and for a few years afterward—exactly the period between his leaving and his writing this letter—the Greek world suffered a severe shortage of grain (the difficult time or present crisis he may have been referring to in 7:26). It was a time of great distress, as much because people were anxious that it would get worse as because of the immediate effects of the crisis.

   What would be some examples of a "very difficult time" in which

Christian believers should put on hold such life-changing plans as marriage?

9. In your everyday life how much thought do you give to the Lord's return, and what are some practical results of your thinking?

I think Paul is referring in 7:29 both to the immediate crisis of the famine and to the fact that it points forward to the ultimate crisis, the time of the Lord's return (1 Corinthians 4:5). He is using the second of these to color in the warnings which apply to the first. Even if the present crisis suddenly passes, if plentiful food again floods the markets of Corinth and everywhere else, there will still be the final crisis to face. There will never be a time when Christians can settle down and treat the world as though it's going to last forever.

The Christian is not to be alarmed by the various turbulent things that happen in the world, nor to be distressed if troubled times mean putting off (for a while or forever) the kind of life and social status that one might otherwise have expected to enjoy. The present world will one day give way to the world that is to be, the world in which Jesus will have completed his kingly work of defeating all hostile powers, including death itself. What will matter then is whether you were faithful to the Lord in whatever circumstances you found yourself.

10. *Read 1 Corinthians 7:32-40.* Keeping in mind that Paul did not aim to place restrictions on the believers (v. 35), what divided loyalties and worries are inherent in Christian marriage, particularly for newly-weds in difficult times?

11. Where have you seen, and perhaps even experienced, a couple stressed by getting married and jumping into a new sphere of Christian work at the same time?

12. What is Paul's goal for each Corinthian Christian, whether married or unmarried?

13. Throughout this passage where does Paul leave room for individual Christian conscience?

PRAY

How and why are you under stress, whether in your marital status or Christian ministry or both? Consider Paul's words, "I want you to be free from worries" (v. 32). Pray for God's peace to rule in your heart. Pray for wisdom to make the right decisions about sexual matters and that you will make those decisions willingly and joyfully.

NOTE ON 1 CORINTHIANS 7:20-24

One of the great achievements of the nineteenth century, largely the work of devout Christians, was the abolition of the slave trade (not that it doesn't continue in other forms; but the conscience of most of the world affirms that slavery is evil). Surely Paul isn't saying that slavery doesn't matter? Some have even used this passage to suggest that Paul gets his moral teaching so badly wrong that we can't trust him on other matters either.

His point is that even the slave/free distinction, central though it was to all ancient society, doesn't matter compared with the status you have in the Messiah. If you were a slave when you became a Christian, you shouldn't be constantly seeking to become free as though everything depends on it. (But, as he says in 7:21, if you can gain your freedom, grab it with both hands.) Likewise, if you were free, you shouldn't enslave yourself to someone. The overall point Paul is trying to make is not that slavery is somehow justified but that, regardless of your social status, your status as a member of the Messiah's people is far more important.

6

MATTERS OF CONSCIENCE

1 Corinthians 8:1—9:27

Western culture tells its own story as the story of developing freedoms. Any attempt to speak of discipline, self-denial or the necessary abandonment of rights is shouted down as a return to the Dark Ages or the Middle Ages (not that those doing the shouting often have much idea what those periods of history were actually like). Paul takes a long time to build up to the point of saying that Christian obedience often means giving up supposed rights and freedoms in order to become the person God means us to become.

OPEN

What freedoms have you willingly given up, and why? What freedoms would you find hardest to give up, and why?

STUDY

1. In the ancient world each town had plenty of shrines to local gods and goddesses, to the great divinities like Apollo or Venus, and in

Paul's day, more and more to the Roman emperor and members of his family. What people mostly did there was to come with animals for sacrifice. As a result, most of the meat available for sale in a city like Corinth would have been offered in sacrifice. The situation was likely to present problems for the newborn Christian church living in the pagan world.

Read 1 Corinthians 8:1-13. Some teachers in Corinth were apparently saying that Christians had a secret "knowledge" that made them immune to what they did or didn't eat. What does Paul mean when he says love is more important than "knowledge" in guiding how Christians should act (8:1-3)?

2. In addition, how does the theological foundation Paul lays down in 8:4-6 deal with the question of eating food offered to idols?

3. Do you feel free to do certain things that other Christians consider wrong, or do you refrain from certain things that other Christians think are okay? Explain.

4. In 8:7, 10, 12, Paul mentions those with a weak conscience. Paul sees the conscience like a sort of internal compass, telling each person what is right and wrong. But the human conscience, like a compass, is a sensitive instrument and can easily malfunction. Reeducating someone's conscience takes time and patience.

Several of the Christians in Corinth, before their conversion (which was quite recent), had been regular worshipers in the shrines of the idols. They knew what went on there. And once you had shared in that dark but powerful world on a regular basis, perhaps for many years, it would be difficult to separate part of i (the neat) from the whole thing. Years of teaching, prayer and wise help would be needed to cope with any element of the old package deal. Otherwise, it would be disturbing to see Christian friends (who didn't have a background of worshiping idols) eating that meat.

How can a supposedly stronger Christian wind up sinning against a weaker Christian today?

5. How would love for others (8:1-3) and knowing God created the world through Jesus (8:4-6) guide Christians in discerning how we should act?

6. *Read 1 Corinthians 9:1-18.* How does Paul establish his status and rights as an apostle in 9:1-12?

7. Why has he decided not to make use of his rights?

8. What rights might we need to be willing to surrender in order to help serve the cause of the gospel?

Paul had been a persecutor of the young church. When Jesus rescued him from the angry and bitter life he had established for himself, it was so as to commission him to announce the good news. Paul was set free in order to do this, and do it he must. His reward was—that he didn't get a reward (9:18)! The paradox of that embodies the paradox of Paul's whole apostleship, the sheer oddity of who he was and what he was doing.

9. *Read 1 Corinthians 9:19-27.* Expand on what Paul means by each of the different ways (9:19-23) in which he would seek to remove barriers to the gospel.

Freedom is important, but in Christian terms it is never the freedom of a subatomic particle, to whiz around in all directions in an apparently random fashion. It is always freedom *for:* for the Messiah, for God's people, for those who need the gospel. Christian freedom is not freedom to do what you like, but freedom *from* all the things that stop you being the person God wants you to be, which is freedom *for* the service of God and the gospel.

10. Consider Paul's statement "I have become all things to all people, so that in all ways I might save some." What examples have you seen of that verse applied in wrong ways and in right ways?

Paul's statement has sometimes been understood as though Paul was a mere pragmatist or spin doctor who twisted his message this way and that to suit different audiences. That's not what he is saying. The message remains constant. It is the messenger who must swallow his pride, who must give up his rights, who must change his freedom into slavery. Woe to those who trim the message so that they don't have to trim themselves.

11. How do the images of a runner and a boxer (9:24-27) reinforce the main points Paul has been making in chapters 8—9?

PRAY

Thank God for the people who followed the apostle Paul's example and gave up rights and freedoms so you could have the opportunity to hear the good news of Christ. Pray about those areas where you find it hardest to think of giving up your rights for the sake of others. Pray about your relationships with Christians whose consciences are either more restrictive or more lax than yours.

Everything to God's Glory

1 Corinthians 10:1—11:1

One of Paul's main aims in this letter is to get the Corinthians to realize where they are on God's timetable. They are like actors who have blundered onto the stage in the middle of a performance and don't even know which act they're in. They need to discover what has happened so far, how the plot is working out and how the people who played these characters in previous acts managed to get things wrong. So he tells them the story of the exodus from Egypt. At least, he tells them certain selected highlights, carefully phrased in such a way as to say "and you, of course, are in more or less the same position now."

OPEN

How have you learned from the example of people in the Bible? Think of two or three who have had a particularly strong influence on your life.

STUDY

1. *Read 1 Corinthians 10:1-13.* During their exodus from Egypt, what privileges did the Israelites enjoy in the wilderness (10:1-4)?

2. How does Paul turn this review of the exodus into a warning?

Christians are enacting the same drama as the children of Israel did. It isn't just a parallel, as though similar events happen over and over again. It is also a sequence. The first exodus established Israel as God's people, but Israel's story led to the decisive, unique events concerning the Messiah Jesus. Now Jesus' people are God's renewed Israel, and all those previous events are coming true in a new way in and through them. Or at least they are supposed to be; but nothing happens automatically in the Christian life.

3. Recall a time that you thought you were doing well as a Christian and then unexpectedly something went wrong. How did you explain this to yourself?

Paul says that you must not presume that because you are baptized Christians, sharing in the community life where the Spirit is known and present, eating and drinking the bread and wine of the Eucharist, that you have automatically reached a level that requires no further moral effort or restraint. Christian sacraments are not magic.

They don't automatically make you holy in all other respects. They don't automatically bring you salvation. On the contrary; precisely because they are huge privileges, they carry corresponding responsibilities.

4. What sorts of desires led to the Israelites' downfall in the wilderness (10:6-10)?

5. What draws Christians away from following God today?

6. There's a wonderful promise in 10:13. When has God clearly provided a way out of temptation for you?

The temptations we run into are the common lot of all human beings. *But God is faithful!*—words to be carved in letters of gold on the memory and imagination of all Christians. He will make a way of avoiding the temptation.

7. *Read 1 Corinthians 10:14—11:1.* What comparisons and contrasts are found in 10:14-22 between the Christian celebration of Communion and eating at a pagan temple?

8. While Paul condemns eating at a pagan temple, he permits eating
    meat offered to idols (10:25-27). What is the difference?

9. Paul once more, as in 1 Corinthians 8, says in 10:23-30 that there
    are times meat offered to idols shouldn't be eaten. What are those
    times?

10. What reasons does he give here for refraining?

There is no such thing as casual worship. The material world, including food and drink, isn't just useful to sustain human and ani-
mal life. It can become the vehicle, the expression, of the god or
goddess, or the God, you are worshiping in eating it. The material
elements of the Christian family meal, the bread and the wine, do
become vessels or vehicles of the personal life of the Messiah himself. Participating in idol worship is, however, quite a different thing
from going to the meat market.

11. What moral gray areas do you find yourself dealing with regularly?

12. What final overall principles does Paul conclude with in 10:31—11:1 to guide Christian behavior in gray areas?

PRAY

Paul advised the Corinthians, "Copy me, just as I'm copying the Messiah." Thank the Lord for people who have given you Christlike examples to copy. Then consider what patterns of your speech or behavior you would *not* want others to copy. Ask the Lord to change you in those areas to conform to the pattern of Christ. Also pray about areas of life in which you feel especially confident that you will not fail. Remember the warning of 10:12 and pray that God will keep you standing upright.

THE WORSHIPING CHURCH

1 Corinthians 11:2-34

Visit a different culture and you will discover many subtle assumptions, pressures and constraints in society, some of which appear in the way people dress and wear their hair. In Western culture, a man wouldn't go to a dinner party wearing a bathing suit, nor would a woman attend a beach picnic wearing a wedding dress. Most Western churches have stopped putting pressure on women to wear hats in church, but nobody thinks it odd that we are still strict about men *not* wearing hats in church. In this Scripture passage we can only guess at the dynamics of the situation, which is of course what historians always do; but I think we can see the main point Paul wanted to make, even if the reasons why he has put it like this are still puzzling.

OPEN

When have you observed (or even been part of) conflict in a church over what is appropriate and what is inappropriate in public worship? How do you determine what is appropriate in public worship?

STUDY

1. In Paul's day, as in many ways in our day, gender was marked by hair and clothing styles. We can tell from statues, vase paintings and other artwork of the period how this worked out in practice. There was social pressure to maintain appropriate distinctions. *Read 1 Corinthians 11:2-16.* What is the basic issue Paul is addressing?

2. The word *head* obviously has a different meaning in 11:3 than it does in the rest of the passage. It likely does not mean "sovereign" but rather "source," as the head or source of a river. While echoes of this are found in verses 8, 9 and 12 where Paul alludes to the creation story in Genesis 2, Paul also notes in verse 12 that men come from women at birth.

   Paul's underlying point seems to be that in worship it is important for both men and women to be their truly created selves, to honor God by being what they are and not blurring the lines by pretending to be something else. God's creation needs humans to be fully, gloriously and truly human, which means fully and truly male and female. In worship men should follow the dress and hair codes which proclaim them to be male, and women the codes which proclaim them to be female. These codes, of course, are different in different cultures. The marks of difference between the sexes should not be set aside in worship.

   While noting differences between men and women, how does Paul also affirm their mutual interdependence (vv. 11-12)?

3. We face different issues, but making sure that our worship is ordered
    appropriately, to honor God's creation and anticipate its fulfillment
    in the new creation, is still a priority. How could your behavior ex-
    press greater honor to God when you enter into worship?

4. Paul now has to tell the Corinthians that, if they have been blurring
    the lines between male and female which should have been clearly
    marked, in another area they are marking out clearly a line which
    should have been obliterated altogether.

    Read 1 Corinthians 11:17-34. What is the division noted in 11:17-22 in
    the Corinthian church that was making things worse, not better?

5. While the Eucharist or Lord's Supper today is generally celebrated as
    a token or symbolic meal, in Corinth it was a full meal that became
    a sign of social divisions. Though such divisions may not be appar-
    ent these days at Communion, where do we see evidence of similar
    divisions in the church?

When the Corinthians came together to celebrate the Lord's meal,
the Supper or Eucharist, they were reinforcing a social distinction
which had nothing to do with God's intention in creation, and nothing to do with God's achievement of salvation through the Messiah.
This is the division between rich and poor, which ran like an ugly
line through ancient society as much as in our own if not more,

and which threatened to deface the very celebration at which the church's unity in the Messiah ought to have been most apparent.

6. In 11:23-34 we have the earliest written record of what happened on the night Jesus was handed over to his death. The Gospels were written later, but they, like Paul, looked back to the very early traditions which the church told and retold as the foundation of their common life.

What can you tell about the importance and meaning of the Lord's Supper from this passage?

7. What are some ways that Christians can eat the bread and drink the cup of the Lord "in an unworthy manner" (v. 27)?

8. How can Christians "test themselves" (v. 28) before participating in the Lord's Supper?

9. When we enact the Lord's Supper we announce Jesus' death (v. 26). Doing it says it. Through Jesus' death the powers are defeated, and people who were enslaved to them are rescued. No wonder the interpretation and practice of the Eucharist has been so controversial in church history. It's an action which speaks louder than words.

Considering this passage as a whole, what changes do you need to make in your attitudes and actions in public worship?

10. What changes might your church need to make in its approach to
worship?

PRAY

Pray that your behavior and thoughts in worship will bring honor to the
Lord rather than dishonor. Ask God to open your eyes to any ways in
which you feel superior toward other believers in your church fellowship. Pray for your church, that all of you together will honor the Lord.
Pray about the next time you take Communion, that you will recognize
the Lord's presence in the bread and the cup.

NOTE ON 1 CORINTHIANS 11:10

Why does Paul say that a woman "must have authority on her head,
because of the angels"? This is one of the most puzzling verses in a
puzzling passage, but there is help of sorts in the Dead Sea Scrolls.
There it is assumed that when God's people meet for worship, the angels
are there too (as many liturgies, and theologians, still affirm). For the
Scrolls, this means that the angels, being holy, must not be offended by
any appearance of unholiness among the congregation, as might be the
case if women in worship uncovered and let down their hair in the manner of the prostitutes of Paul's day.

When humans are renewed in the Messiah and raised from the dead,
they will be set in authority over the angels (1 Corinthians 6:3). In worship, the church anticipates how things are going to be in that new day.

When a woman is praying or prophesying (perhaps in the language of angels, as in 1 Corinthians 13:1), she needs to be truly what she is, since it is to male and female alike, in their mutual interdependence as God's image-bearing creatures, that the world, including the angels, is to be subject. God's creation needs humans to be fully, gloriously and truly human, which means fully and truly male and female.

LIFE IN THE
BODY OF CHRIST

1 Corinthians 12:1—13:13

One of the most exciting experiences of my teenage years was playing in an orchestra at school. I had learned the piano for a year or two, but you normally play piano without other musicians joining in. Now I began the trombone. Of course when you start an instrument you have to learn and practice by yourself. But then one day you get to sit with forty or fifty others and discover that though you're all playing different instruments, and most of you are playing different parts, it all fits together and—if everyone is doing what they should!—it makes a wonderful combined sound.

The problem Paul now confronts in Corinth is that within the Christian orchestra there were some who considered themselves superior to others, and there was a danger as a result that the whole symphony might be played out of balance and even out of tune.

OPEN

What are different ways *spiritual* is defined by people who aren't Christians?

STUDY

1. *Read 1 Corinthians 12:1-20.* A word used in verse 1 is sometimes translated "spiritual gifts" but it more accurately just means "spiritual things." Paul does use the word *gifts* in verse 4, usually understood as "spiritual gifts" or "gifts from God through the working of the Holy Spirit."

   According to what Paul says in 12:1-11, what is the point of spiritual gifts?

2. Paul emphasizes that the source of spiritual gifts is the Spirit. What then is he implying is not the source, and why is that important?

3. We speak of being a church *member* without thinking about where the word comes from. The word *member* owes its place in Christian thinking and speaking largely to 1 Corinthians 12:12-20 where the word means *limb* or *organ*. We might expect Paul to say in 12:12 "as the body is one, and has many members . . . so also is *the church.*" Instead he says "so also is *the Messiah.*"

   When you think of yourself as a member of Christ himself, what comes to mind?

4. How does thinking of other Christians as members of Christ himself affect the way you see them?

5. *Read 1 Corinthians 12:21-31.* What sorts of "body parts" in the church do Christians tend to regard as more important than others?

6. What are some practical ways you have seen 12:26 in action?

Paul undermines actual or potential boasting in the church by insisting that every single member of the body is just as indispensable as any other. He insists on equality between different functions, leaving no room for social, cultural or spiritual elitism or snobbery within the church. He wants every Christian in Corinth to value every other Christian and care for him or her, just like the hand comes to bandage the injured foot, or the foot hurries to take the injured head to the hospital.

7. How can Christians be connected not only with members of their local fellowship but with Christians around the globe?

8. First Corinthians 28-30 is one of several scriptural lists of spiritual gifts. (Others are in Romans 12:6-8 and Ephesians 4:11.) The lists

differ from each other with some overlap. What does this rich diversity of gifts say to you about the Holy Spirit's work in the church?

9. *Read 1 Corinthians 12:31—13:13.* Many people know 1 Corinthians 13 through being read at weddings as though it was a detached poem. It is more like the slow movement of a symphony whose first movement is chapter 12 and whose final movement is chapter 14— the symphony of Paul's teaching about the corporate worship of the church, especially about the use of different gifts by different members of the worshiping congregation.

Consider the things which Paul calls *less* important than love (13:1-3). How are each of these connected to the topics mentioned in chapters 11 and 12?

10. How do the attitudes and outlook in 13:4-7 compare with the values of the world?

11. In chapter 13 Paul presents the life which will bring the right sort of order to the chaos of faction-fighting and spiritual jealousy within the church. This life is within the reach of every one of us because it is the life of Jesus, the life inspired by the Spirit, the life which is our birthright within the Messiah's body.

How might you put some aspect of this description of love into action in your Christian fellowship?

12. What does 13:8-13 promise about the future?

13. Why do you think love is greater than either faith or hope (13:13)?

PRAY

Pray for yourself, that you will more consistently speak and act in love within the body of Christ. Pray for your fellow Christians, that you will esteem them as fellow members of the body. Pray that your church will be marked by love rather than pride, ambition or conflict. Thank God for his grace in Jesus, which covers your own failures and those of your fellow believers.

PRIORITIES IN WORSHIP

1 Corinthians 14:1-40

Paul now focuses on a specific issue which, though at one level it simply relates to the ordering of public worship, at another level goes near the heart of what he wants to say to the Corinthians. The contrast is between the person who builds up their private spirituality and the person who, in public worship, builds up the whole community. Paul has nothing against private spirituality, but he is aware of its dangers. The problem centers on two "gifts" from among those he listed in chapter 12. The key question is: are you behaving according to the principle of chapter 13? Are you exercising the gifts God gives you in the spirit of love?

OPEN

Think about your experience when your church comes together for corporate worship. Would you say that it is geared toward building up each person's private spirituality or geared toward building up the entire body? Why do you answer that way?

STUDY

1. *Read 1 Corinthians 14:1-19.* Tongues refers to the gift of speech which, using apparent or even actual languages, the speaker never learned. It is experienced as a stream of praise in which a sense of love for God, of adoration and gratitude, wells up and overflows like a private language of love. *Prophecy* is more than foretelling the future or receiving sudden flashes of inspiration; it is God-given wisdom, understanding, insight and teaching.

   How, in 14:1-5, does Paul contrast the use of tongues and prophecy in public worship in the church?

2. What reason does Paul give to be "more delighted" to have the Corinthians prophesy in public than to speak in tongues in public?

   The underlying contrast here is the same as we saw in 1 Corinthians 8:1-2. There are some things which can "puff you up," making you proud and self-important, but what *builds* people up is love. And this chapter is all about making sure that public worship builds everybody up rather than everybody developing their own spiritual giftedness and displaying it like so many strutting peacocks. When people come together to worship God revealed in Jesus, they are not building their own private houses. They are building a great cathedral for all to share and enjoy.

3. The danger for those who are eager to use their new gifts in public is that they will forget the real point of coming together, which is

that the church family as a whole should be built up. If the message spoken by a believer is indistinct or unintelligible, what will be the results (vv. 6-12)?

4. How is what Paul says here relevant to much wider issues in corporate worship than simply speaking in tongues?

5. How is the mind of the worshiper to be involved in worship (vv. 13-19)?

6. Paul makes an extreme statement in verse 19. What do his words reveal to you about what he considered important and valuable in the church?

Rooted as he was in Jewish thinking, Paul saw a human being as a rich, many-sided, complicated but integrated whole. For him *body, mind, heart, soul* and *spirit* were not words to describe different parts that you could separate. They were words to describe *the whole person seen from one angle*. In particular, *spirit* describes the whole person at his or her deepest level of consciousness, which is in fact linked in a thousand ways to mind, heart and body. And *mind* describes the whole person as a thinking, reasoning being, which is again linked to everything else we are and do. When you look at a worshiping Christian, you should see a whole human being with every aspect united in giving praise to God.

7. Paul himself clearly still uses the gift of tongues in his personal and private prayers, and he doesn't see this as a sign of immaturity (v. 18). Maturity comes in knowing what behavior is appropriate in which context.

   Read 1 Corinthians 14:20-40. How can Christians be children in regard to evil but still be adults in their thinking (v. 20)?

8. What does Paul say will be the contrasting reactions of unbelievers who come into an assembly where Christians are speaking in tongues and where they are prophesying?

9. What does this contrast tell us about the priorities Paul sees in worship?

10. How does Paul expand on what it means to build each other up in worship in 14:29-31?

11. When worship is chaotic or filled with strife, what harm can be done to the body of Christ?

Verses 34-35 are odd because in 1 Corinthians 11:2-16 Paul assumes that women will take leadership roles in praying and prophesying. There are several scenarios which might explain the sudden need for a commandment of this type. What is clear is that this is a particular problem posed from within the cultural setting of the time, and Paul's overriding concern is for order, peace and mutual upbuilding when the congregation comes together for worship, rather than for chaos, interruption and dissension.

12. If Christians are to behave as Paul describes throughout 1 Corinthians 14, what attitudes must they bring to public worship?

PRAY

Pray that God will develop attitudes in you which will make you a blessing to the entire body when you meet for worship. Pray that you will know when to speak and when to keep silent. Pray also for sincere love for your brothers and sisters in Christ.

RISEN AND REIGNING

1 Corinthians 15:1-28

This chapter in 1 Corinthians is one of the greatest sustained discussions of a topic which Paul ever wrote. The theme is the resurrection—the resurrection of Jesus and the future resurrection of those who believe in Jesus. Some in Corinth have a problem with this; but there is a much wider reason why Paul gives the topic such a lengthy treatment and places it here as the final major theme of the letter. We have seen over and over again that he is trying to get the Corinthians to understand where they are and who they are in God's long story. If they understand where they belong in this story, so many other things that have troubled them will be seen in the correct light.

OPEN

What are your thoughts and feelings and experiences with death?

STUDY

1. *Read 1 Corinthians 15:1-11.* What is the essence of what Paul had "handed on" to the Corinthians?

2. Why do you think Paul bothered to list the various people, including himself, who had seen the risen Jesus?

We need to be clear about what the word *resurrection* meant for Paul and his hearers. It didn't mean "life after death." It was never a general term for any and every belief about what might happen to people after they die. Nobody in Corinth would have thought Paul meant simply that Jesus had gone after his death into some kind of glorious but non-bodily existence. *Resurrection* meant, very specifically, that people already dead would be given new bodies, would return to an embodied life not completely unlike the one they had had before.

3. How did Paul's life demonstrate the extent of God's grace?

Paul wants to be clear that the resurrection is rock-bottom reality for the Christian. It isn't a strange idea that he has dreamed up himself. He and all the others tell the same story; it has already become a carefully guarded tradition (vv. 1, 3, 11). The story forms the gospel, the announcement of the good news of Jesus the Messiah. The only point in being a Christian at all is if this message continues to be the solid ground on which you stand.

4. *Read 1 Corinthians 15:12-19.* Paul's careful argument in this section is designed to show the Corinthians, starkly, what would follow if you were to declare that there is no resurrection. What would be the consequences if Christ was not raised from the dead?

5. Why is the Corinthians' faith—and our faith—"pointless" if the Messiah has not been raised (v. 17)?

6. Christians have always testified and continue to testify that Christ gives them peace, hope and many other benefits in this present life. Why then do you think Paul would make such an extreme statement as verse 19?

7. *Read 1 Corinthians 15:20-28.* This passage is near the heart of Paul's understanding of Jesus, God, history and the world. It's near the heart of what Jesus himself spent his short public career talking about. It's about the coming of God's kingdom. What is the "proper order" (vv. 23-24) of the stages of the coming of the kingdom?

Many Jews of Paul's day longed for God to restore Israel to glory, defeat the nations that had oppressed it and raise all the righteous dead to share in the new world. They didn't all agree on exactly how this would happen, but they knew somehow, at the end of history, all God's people would be raised. Instead, shockingly, unexpectedly, one person was raised in the middle of history.

8. "Death is the last enemy to be destroyed" (v. 26). In what ways is death an *enemy?*

9. How does the resurrection show the defeat of death?

10. What difference does this make as we grieve for those who have died and as we contemplate our own death?

11. What insights about resurrection have you drawn from 1 Corinthians 15 so far?

PRAY

"If the Messiah wasn't raised, your faith is pointless, and you are still in your sins. . . . But in fact the Messiah has been raised from the dead, as the first fruits of those who have fallen asleep" (vv. 17, 20). If you have put your faith in the risen Messiah, praise God that he has dealt with your sins and that you have the sure hope of resurrection. If you still have doubts, bring them freely and boldly to God and invite him to deal with them—and with you.

12

BODILY TRANSFORMATION

1 Corinthians 15:29-58

Christianity isn't a philosophy, a set of ideas. It isn't a path of spirituality. It isn't a rule of life. It isn't a political agenda. It includes and indeed gives energy to all those things; but at its very heart it is something different. It is good news about an event which has happened in the world, an event because of which the world can never be the same again. And those who believe it and live by it will never be the same again either. That's what 1 Corinthians 15 is all about.

OPEN

Besides its many blessings, the Christian life also includes struggles and difficulties. Think of a struggle you have experienced (or are experiencing) in your Christian life. What made (or is making) the struggle worthwhile?

STUDY

1. Paul was good at breaking up a heavy discussion with a change of pace and style, and that's what he does next. *Read 1 Corinthians 15:29-34.* The question of being "baptized on behalf of the dead" (v. 29) has long been a puzzle. Whatever it means, it was something the Corinthians knew about as a regular practice, and it made no sense unless there was in fact a resurrection to look forward to.

   If death is the end, with no resurrection, what does Paul say is the logical conclusion about how we might as well live our everyday lives?

2. Paul refers to fighting wild animals at Ephesus (v. 32). Acts 19 describes Paul's ministry at Ephesus, but there is no evidence that he fought wild animals in an arena as gladiators would have done. I am inclined to think that he refers metaphorically to the enormous opposition that the gospel aroused in Ephesus from those who saw it as a political, economic and religious threat. Paul says that if he went through all that only to die, with no hope of resurrection, he would be just like the gladiators, eating, drinking and making merry the night before the big show, knowing that this was the end.

   How does the resurrection make sense of the sacrifices we make as Christians?

3. What difference can the reality of the resurrection make in our everyday life and thinking?

4. *Read 1 Corinthians 15:35-49*. How does Paul say nature itself illustrates the transformation from the old body to the resurrection body?

5. Many versions of the Bible translate the words in 15:44 as "physical body" and "spiritual body," but this is highly misleading. Paul is not making a contrast between our physical self and our spiritual self, something we might call a ghost. The contrast he's making is between a body *animated by* one type of life and a body animated by another type. One is animated by food, drink and air, the other by God's own Spirit.

   How does this help us understand the practical difference the resurrection should make in our lives?

6. By mentioning Adam and plants, animals, birds, fish as well as the sun and moon, Paul is calling to mind Genesis 1. What is he trying to communicate about the resurrection by doing so?

7. In 15:49 he makes one more reference to Genesis 1, this time to 1:26-28, the climax of creation. What does Paul mean when he says we will bear the likeness or image "of the man from heaven"?

8. *Read 1 Corinthians 15:50-58.* What does Paul say will happen to believers who have died when the Lord appears?

9. There is one apparent problem remaining: what happens to those who are still alive when the Lord appears, since "we won't all sleep" (v. 51)? What does Paul say about them?

10. You might think, after a spectacular chapter like this one, that Paul would conclude by saying something like "So let's rejoice at the wonderful hope we can look forward to!" But he doesn't. What does he do instead in verse 58 and why?

11. Do you ever suspect that the work you are doing for the Lord is futile or too small to make a difference? How can verse 58 be an encouragement for you in those times?

PRAY

The truth of the resurrection of the dead and the transformation of the living is not just a truth about the future hope. It's a truth about the present significance of what we are and do. If it is true that God is going to transform this present world and renew our whole selves, bodies included, then what we do in the present time with our bodies, and with our world, matters.

Thank God for the hope of transformation. Pray that you will be energized by the confidence that God will have the last say and the final victory over weakness and corruption. Pray that you will be "firmly fixed, unshakeable, always full to overflowing with the Lord's work" (v. 58).

NOTE ON 1 CORINTHIANS 15:29

Regarding the "baptism for the dead," it may be that some Christians had died without being baptized, and that the practice had grown up (if so it didn't last long) of other people undergoing baptism on their behalf as a sign and symbol that they really did belong to the Messiah. Or it may be that "being baptized on behalf of the dead" refers to non-Christians who, after the death of close relatives or friends who were Christians, decided to become Christians themselves, undergoing baptism so that they would continue to be with their loved ones in the final resurrection.

13

DO EVERYTHING WITH LOVE

1 Corinthians 16:1-24

This letter to the Christians at Corinth, which has addressed the problem of divisions within the church, and of the urgent need for love at the heart of everything, brings it all into focus with a practical hard-headed scheme. The church in Jerusalem had suffered grievously by persecution, the scattering of its members and perhaps also from the enthusiastic pooling of resources in its early days. Now Paul has developed a plan for a monetary collection as a long-term strategy for making both sides of the great ethnic divide in the early church, Jew and Gentile, understand the truth of the matter.

He wants to signal to the Gentile Christians that they are part of the same family as the Jewish Christians in Jerusalem. Likewise he wants the Jewish Christians to know that those Gentiles out there, who have come to faith in Jesus as the Messiah and the true Lord of the world, are part of the same family even though they haven't become Jews in the process.

OPEN

Think of the members of your Christian fellowship. What holds all of you together?

STUDY

1. *Read 1 Corinthians 16:1-9.* How does Paul affirm his own relationship with the Corinthians even as he makes plans for collecting and delivering relief to the Jerusalem church?

2. After the lofty tone and subject of chapter 15—the hope of resurrection—are you surprised at the sudden shift to "the collection for God's people" in this chapter? Why or why not?

3. In 16:9 Paul mentions an "open door" and "opposition." Where the gospel is preached, why do these often go together?

4. *Read 1 Corinthians 16:10-24.* Timothy was considerably younger than Paul, and Paul refers to him as working with him like a son with his father—this in a world where sons were regularly apprenticed to fathers (1 Corinthians 4:17; see also Philippians 2:22). But Timothy seems not to have been what we would call a forceful personality. How would the coming of Timothy test the Corinthians in the issues that Paul has been writing about in this letter?

5. The church at Corinth was marked by party spirit, and Apollos had

his own group of loyal followers (1 Corinthians 1:12). How does Paul defuse any sense of competition between himself and Apollos?

6. The four commands in verse 13 correspond to what an army commander might say to someone on guard. How do you or your church need to keep alert, stand firm in the faith, be brave and be strong?

7. "*Whatever* you do, do it with love" (v. 14). As you think about a difficult situation you face right now, what would it mean to approach that situation with love?

8. Stephanas, Fortunatus and Achaicus have brought Paul the letter from the Corinthian church, and they have stayed with him while he has pondered it and dictated his reply. Priscilla (also called Prisca) and Aquila had been part of the Corinthian church from its earliest days (Acts 18).

How do the final lines of the letter in 16:15-24 serve to stitch together Paul's connections with the Corinthians, not in general but in specific ways?

9. Paul had been dictating this letter to another who wrote it down.

In verses 21-24 he takes the pen, as we do today after dictating or typing a letter, both to write a signature and add a few closing remarks—which, of course, gain all the more significance both by coming at the end and by being in his own hand. What is the focus of his final words?

10. How are these final words appropriate given the major themes Paul has covered in this letter?

11. Looking back on the entire letter of 1 Corinthians, where have you been most challenged, reassured or strengthened?

PRAY

Thank God for preserving this letter to the ancient church in Corinth and making it available for you to read, study and put into practice. Keep praying that all you do will be done in love. From the heart pray *Marana tha*, "Our Lord, come!"

GUIDELINES FOR LEADERS

My grace is sufficient for you.
(2 Corinthians 12:9)

If leading a small group is something new for you, don't worry. These sessions are designed to flow naturally and be led easily. You may even find that the studies seem to lead themselves!

This study guide is flexible. You can use it with a variety of groups—students, professionals, coworkers, friends, neighborhood or church groups. Each study takes forty-five to sixty minutes in a group setting.

You don't need to be an expert on the Bible or a trained teacher to lead a small group. These guides are designed to facilitate a group's discussion, not a leader's presentation. Guiding group members to discover together what the Bible has to say and to listen together for God's guidance will help them remember much more than a lecture would.

There are some important facts to know about group dynamics and encouraging discussion. The suggestions listed below should equip you to effectively and enjoyably fulfill your role as leader.

PREPARING FOR THE STUDY

1. Ask God to help you understand and apply the passage in your own life. Unless this happens, you will not be prepared to lead others. Pray too for the various members of the group. Ask God to open

your hearts to the message of his Word and motivate you to action.

2. Read the introduction to the entire guide to get an overview of the topics that will be explored.

3. As you begin each study, read and reread the assigned Bible passage to familiarize yourself with it. This study guide is based on the For Everyone series on the New Testament (published by SPCK and Westminster John Knox). It will help you and the group if you have on hand a copy of the companion volume from the For Everyone series both for the translation of the passage found there and for further insight into the passage.

4. Carefully work through each question in the study. Spend time in meditation and reflection as you consider how to respond.

5. Write your thoughts and responses in the space provided in the study guide. This will help you to express your understanding of the passage clearly.

6. It may help to have a Bible dictionary handy. Use it to look up any unfamiliar words, names or places. The glossary at the end of each New Testament for Everyone commentary may likewise be helpful for keeping discussion moving.

7. Reflect seriously on how you need to apply the Scripture to your life. Remember that the group members will follow your lead in responding to the studies. They will not go any deeper than you do.

LEADING THE STUDY

1. At the beginning of your first time together, explain that these studies are meant to be discussions, not lectures. Encourage the members of the group to participate. However, do not put pressure on those who may be hesitant to speak—especially during the first few sessions.

2. Be sure that everyone in your group has a study guide. Encourage the group to prepare beforehand for each discussion by reading the introduction to the guide and by working through the questions in each study.

3. Begin each study on time. Open with prayer, asking God to help the group to understand and apply the passage.

4. Have a group member read aloud the introduction at the beginning of the discussion.

5. Discuss the "Open" question before the Bible passage is read. The "Open" question introduces the theme of the study and helps group members to begin to open up, and can reveal where our thoughts and feelings need to be transformed by Scripture. Reading the passage first will tend to color the honest reactions people would otherwise give—because they are, of course, supposed to think the way the Bible does. Encourage as many members as possible to respond to the "Open" question, and be ready to get the discussion going with your own response.

6. Have a group member read aloud the passage to be studied as indicated in the guide.

7. The study questions are designed to be read aloud just as they are written. You may, however, prefer to express them in your own words.

   There may be times when it is appropriate to deviate from the study guide. For example, a question may have already been answered. If so, move on to the next question. Or someone may raise an important question not covered in the guide. Take time to discuss it, but try to keep the group from going off on tangents.

8. Avoid answering your own questions. An eager group quickly becomes passive and silent if members think the leader will do most of the talking. If necessary repeat or rephrase the question until it is clearly understood, or refer to the commentary woven into the guide to clarify the context or meaning.

9. Don't be afraid of silence in response to the discussion questions. People may need time to think about the question before formulating their answers.

10. Don't be content with just one answer. Ask, "What do the rest of you think?" or "Anything else?" until several people have given answers to the question.

11. Try to be affirming whenever possible. Affirm participation. Never reject an answer; if it is clearly off-base, ask, "Which verse led you to that conclusion?" or again, "What do the rest of you think?"

12. Don't expect every answer to be addressed to you, even though this will probably happen at first. As group members become more at ease, they will begin to truly interact with each other. This is one sign of healthy discussion.

13. Don't be afraid of controversy. It can be very stimulating. If you don't resolve an issue completely, don't be frustrated. Explain that the group will move on and God may enlighten all of you in later sessions.

14. Periodically summarize what the group has said about the passage. This helps to draw together the various ideas mentioned and gives continuity to the study. But don't preach.

15. Conclude your time together with the prayer suggestion at the end of the study, adapting it to your group's particular needs as appropriate. Ask for God's help in following through on the applications you've identified.

16. End on time.

Many more suggestions and helps for studying a passage or guiding discussion can be found in *How to Lead a LifeGuide Bible Study* and *The Big Book on Small Groups* (both from InterVarsity Press/USA).

Other InterVarsity Press Resources from N. T. Wright

The Challenge of Jesus
N. T. Wright offers clarity and a full accounting of the facts of the life and teachings of Jesus, revealing how the Son of God was also solidly planted in first-century Palestine. *978-0-8308-2200-3, 202 pages, hardcover*

Resurrection
This 50-minute DVD confronts the most startling claim of Christianity—that Jesus rose from the dead. Shot on location in Israel, Greece and England, N. T. Wright presents the political, historical and theological issues of Jesus' day and today regarding this claim. Wright brings clarity and insight to one of the most profound mysteries in human history. Study guide included.
978-0-8308-3435-8, DVD

Evil and the Justice of God
N. T. Wright explores all aspects of evil and how it presents itself in society today. Fully grounded in the story of the Old and New Testaments, this presentation is provocative and hopeful; a fascinating analysis of and response to the fundamental question of evil and justice that faces believers.
978-0-8308-3398-6, 176 pages, hardcover

Evil
Filmed in Israel, South Africa and England, this 50-minute DVD confronts some of the major "evil" issues of our time—from tsunamis to AIDS—and puts them under the biblical spotlight. N. T. Wright says there is a solution to the problem of evil, if only we have the honesty and courage to name it and understand it for what it is. Study guide included. *978-0-8308-3434-1, DVD*

Justification: God's Plan and Paul's Vision
In this comprehensive account and defense of the crucial doctrine of justification, Wright also responds to critics who have challenged what has come to be called the new perspective. Ultimately, he provides a chance for those in the middle of and on both sides of the debate to interact directly with his views and form their own conclusions. *978-0 8308-3863-9, 279 pages, hardcover*

Colossians and Philemon
In Colossians, Paul presents Christ as "the firstborn over all creation," and appeals to his readers to seek a maturity found only Christ. In Philemon, Paul appeals to a fellow believer to receive a runaway slave in love and forgiveness. In this volume N. T. Wright offers comment on both of these important books. *978-0-8308-4242-1, 199 pages, paperback*